RED

by Melanie Mitchell

first step nonfiction

Lerner Publications · Minneapolis

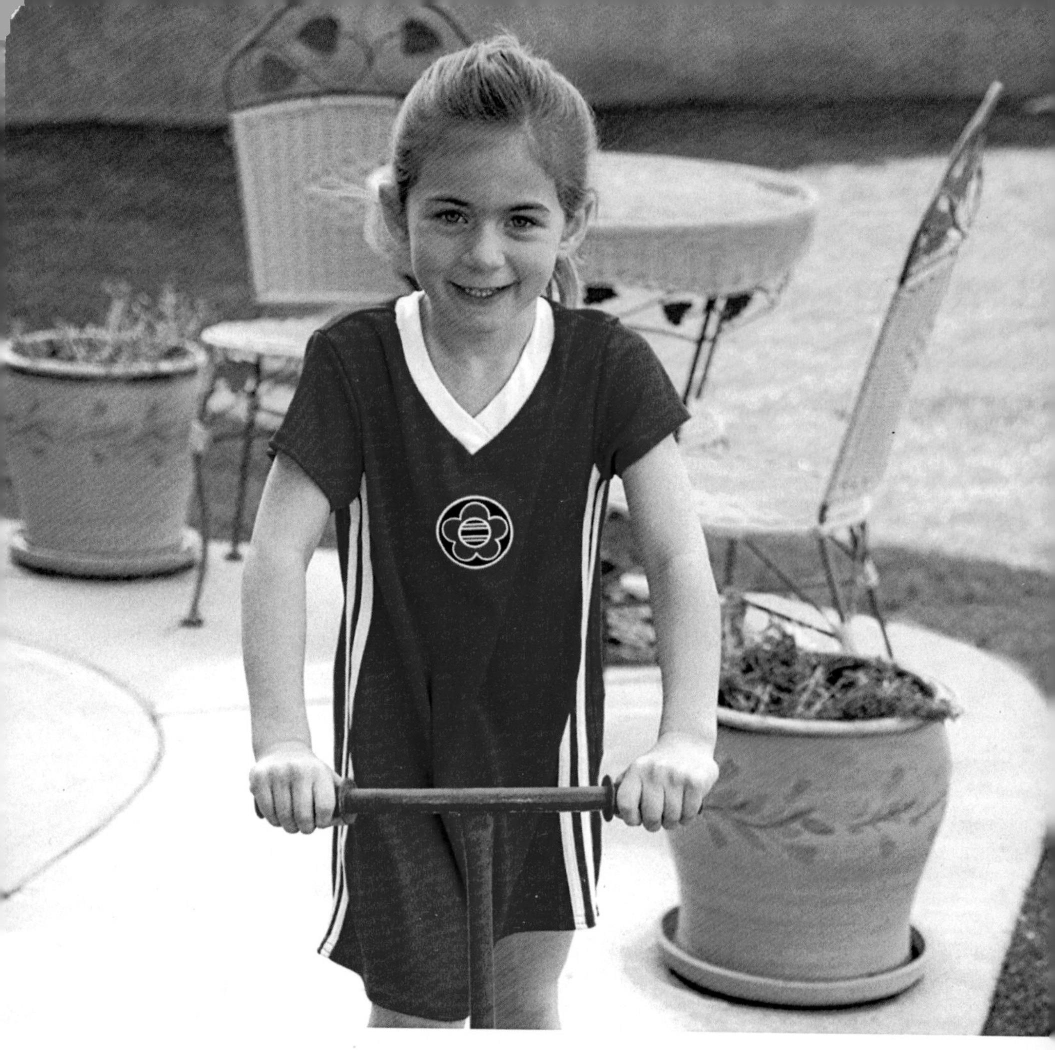

I see red.

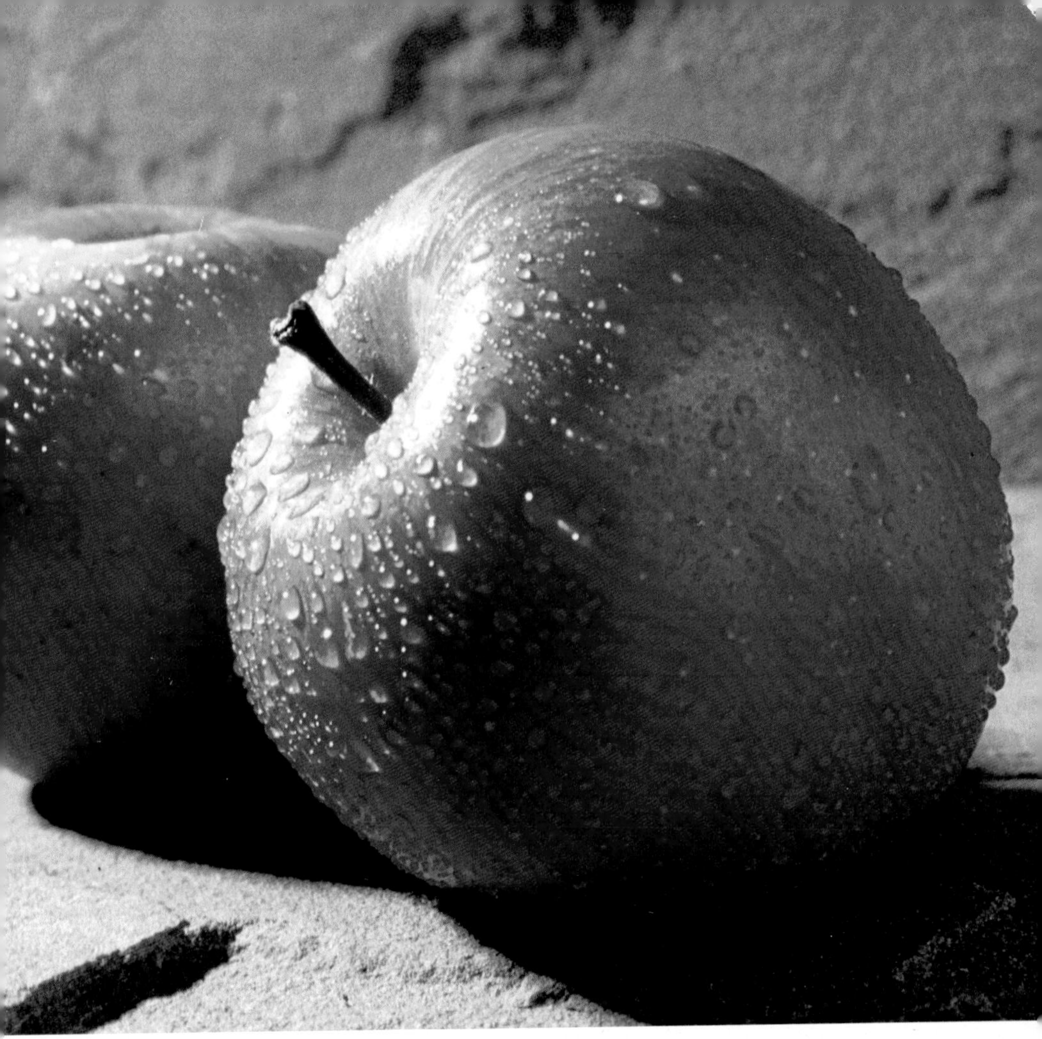

The apple is red.

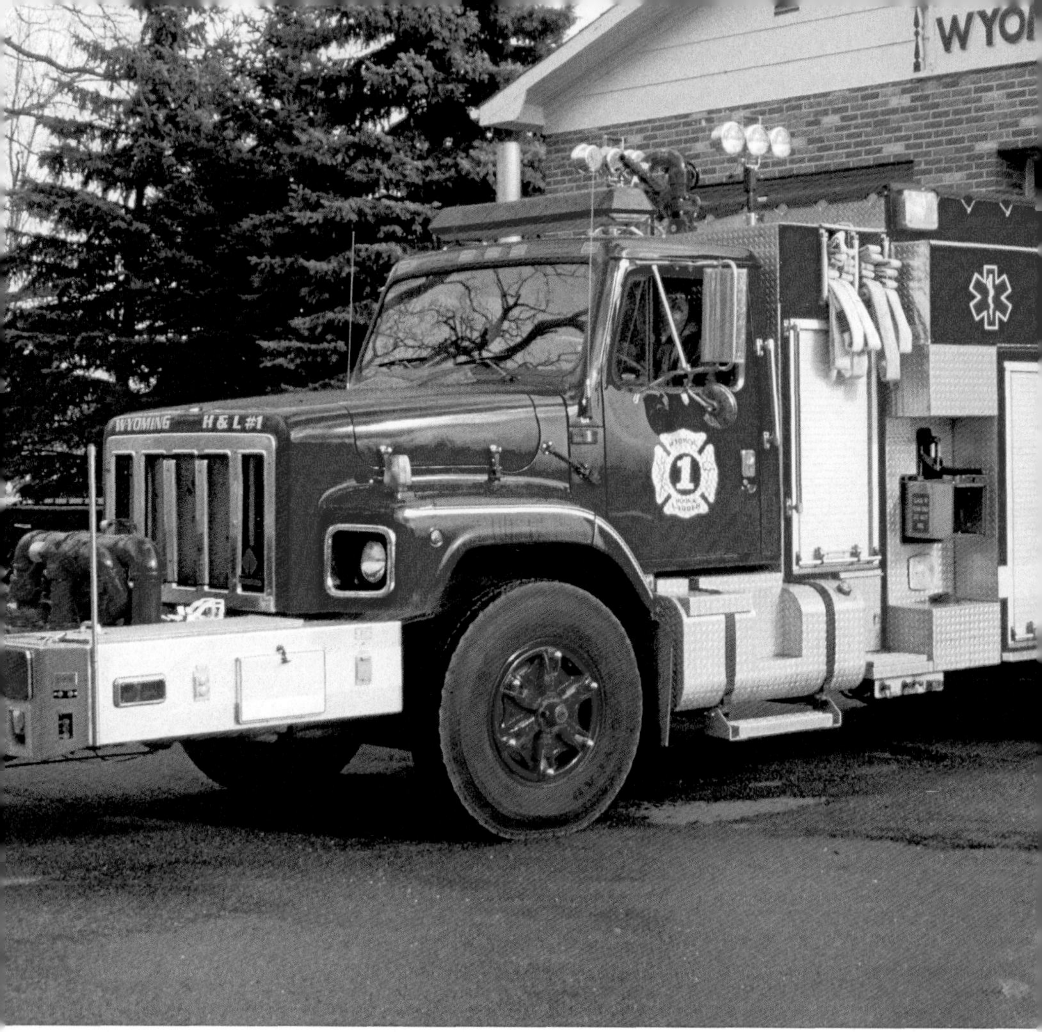

The truck is red.

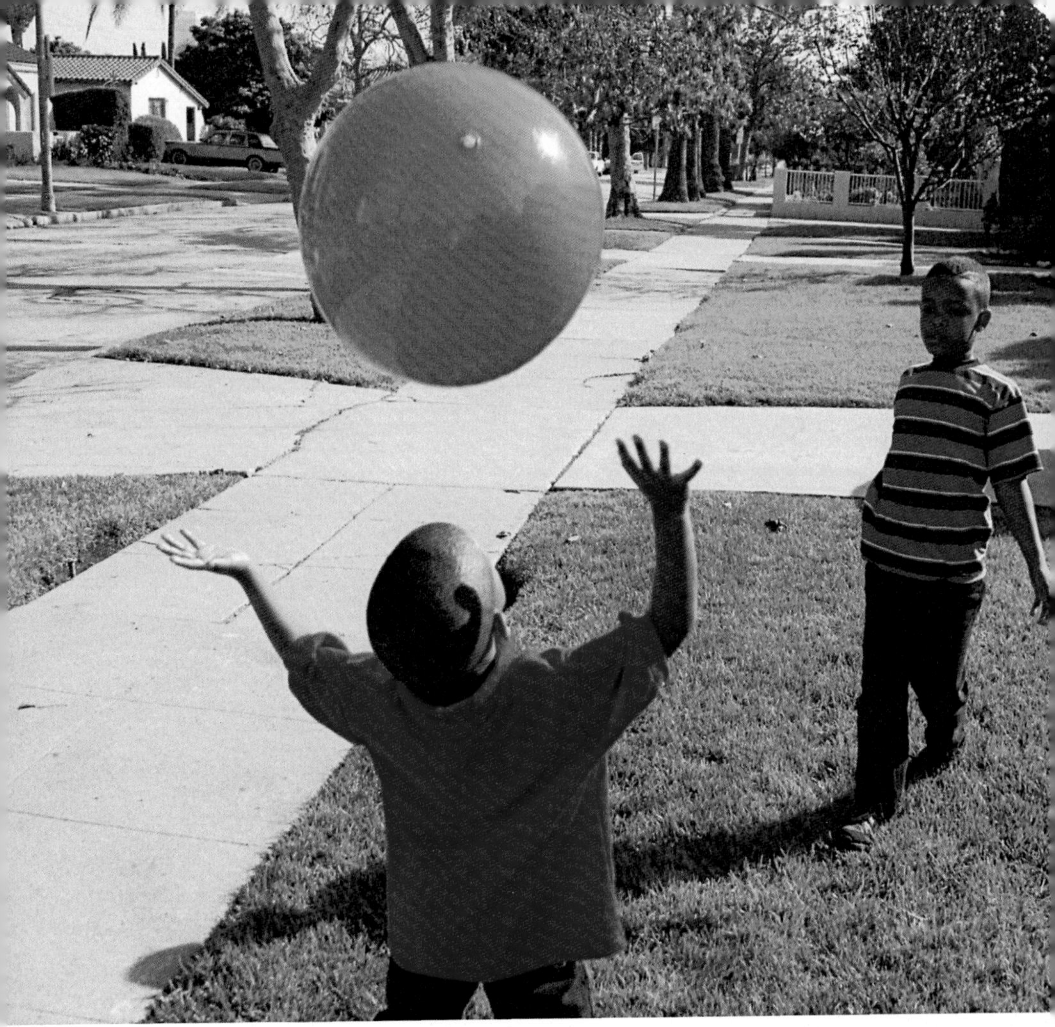

The ball is red.

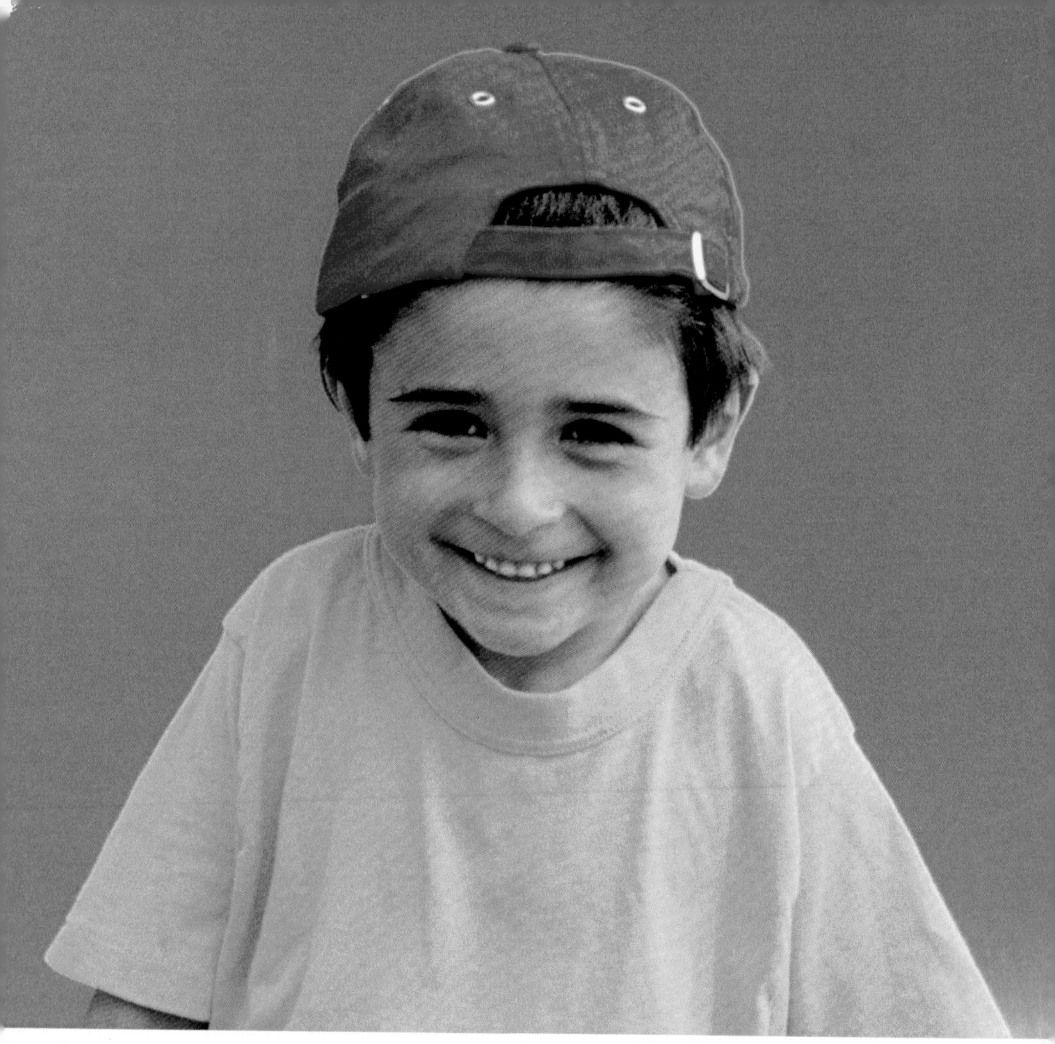

The cap is red.

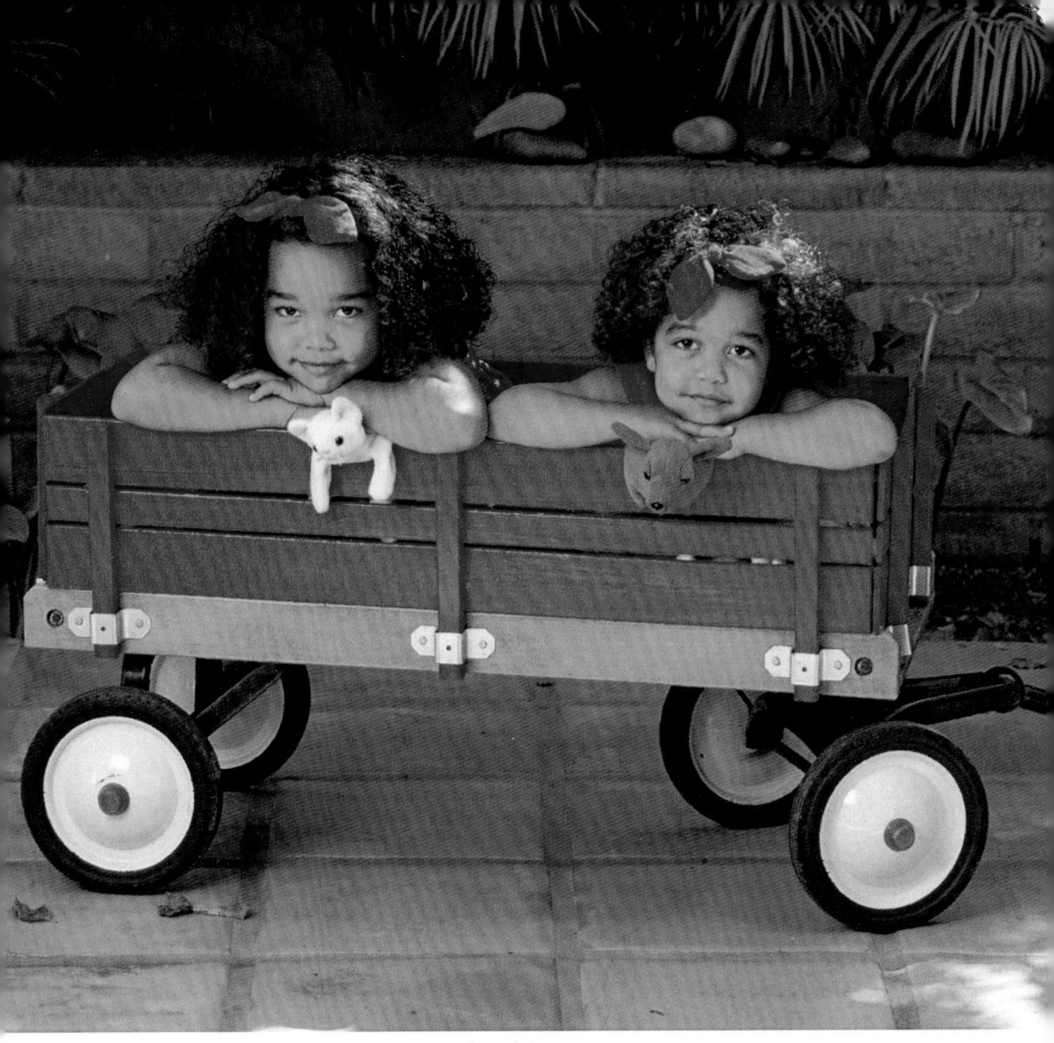

The wagon is red.

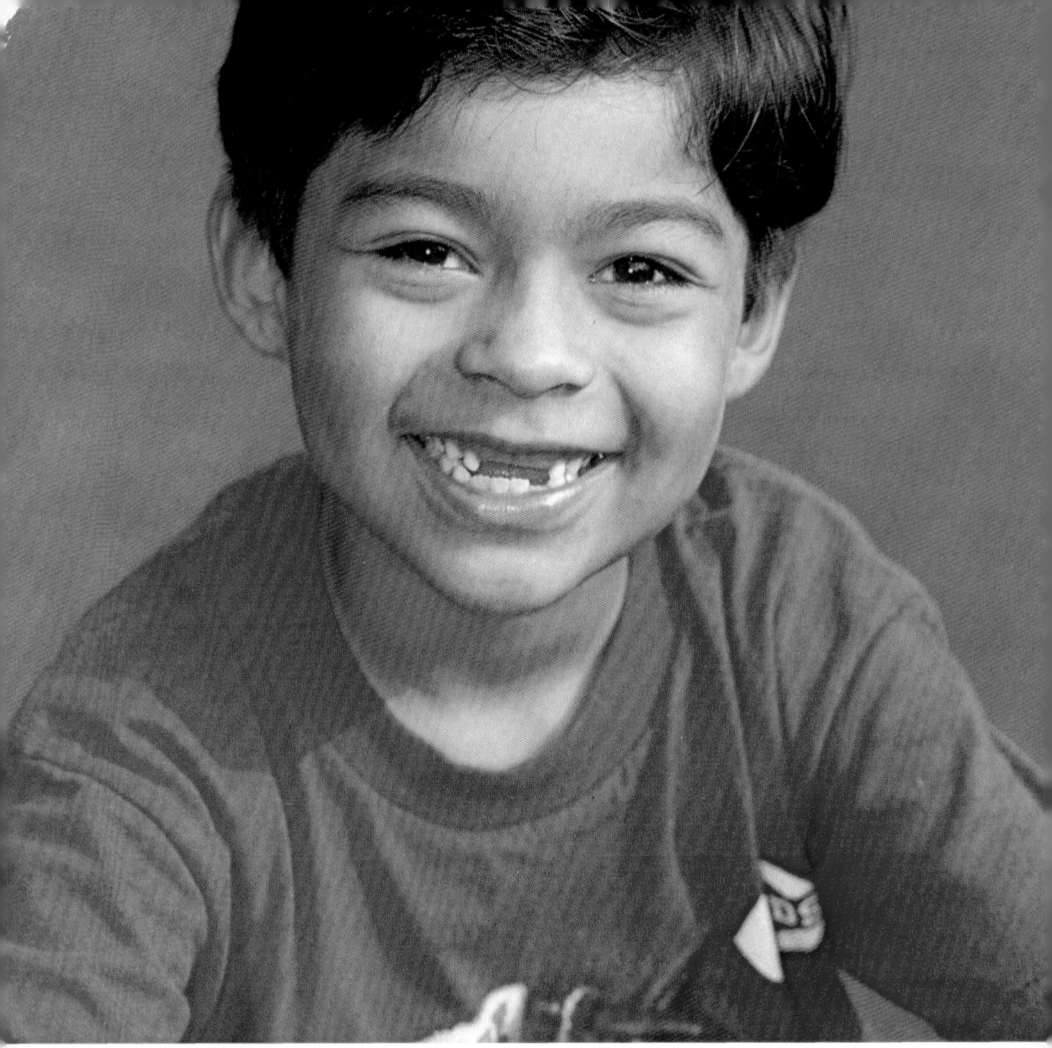

I like red!